Reach your financial and life goals using the T.E.R.M. analysis techniques today.

15 Key Steps to Getting Stuff Done Now!

In order to be productive and get stuff done, you need to be targeted and effective in your approach to the problem. Solve what needs to be solved and nothing more.

With this Itty Bitty® book you will:

- Understand that you need to get out of your own way.
- Break down and manage the goals you truly desire to attain.
- Set targets and hit them with a bull's-eye.
- Have the basic tools to create a happier life for yourself and your family.

Pick up a copy of this powerful Itty Bitty® Book today, set your goals, use the T.E.R.M system and achieve the results you desire.

Your Amazing Itty Bitty® Productivity Book

15 Key Steps to Getting Stuff Done Now!

Matt Malouf

This book is dedicated to my loving and supportive family Gladys, Cally, Elon, Drew, Edward, and Roxxane whose support and love inspire me to reach for better every day. I love you guys so much, words simply can't do it justice

Thank you to all my extended family and friends whose love, support, and contributions would be a book series all their own. You know who you are, and I am forever grateful, you have helped make my dreams a reality.

Stop by our Itty Bitty® website to find to interesting blog entries regarding ……….

www.IttyBittyPublishing.com

Or visit Matt Malouf at

https://www.InvestWithMatt.com

Table of Contents

Introduction

Hello and thank you for allowing me to share with you how I gained peace and clarity in my life while turbocharging my retirement planning while designing my lifestyle. I have so much to share with you! Before getting started just a bit about how my proprietary T.E.R.M. Analysis techniques have helped me create.

1. I own 28 properties in four different countries with only a single mortgage so far.
2. I was able to build my retirement portfolio part-time in the evenings by being targeted productive.
3. I'm a renowned expert in my profession of Traffic Management.
4. I believe helping others turbocharge their lifestyle will make the world a better place.
5. In order to be productive and get stuff done, you need to be targeted and effective in your approach to the problem. Solve what needs to be solved and nothing more. I will help you with this.

By the time you finish this book you will:

- Understand that you need to get out of your own way.

- Break down and manage the goals you truly desire to attain.
- Set targets and hit them with a bullseye.
- Have the basic tools to create a happier life for yourself and your family.

Remember that we tend to overcomplicate all aspects of our life. This will help you hyper-focus and target what needs to be solved and hitting it hard to solve it. We do this, simply and effectively, through the TERM Methodology that you will learn here.

This process can be used for anything such as real estate investment, business marketing courses, new joint ventures, adding a side hustle, losing weight, and more; the list goes on.

Reading this book will change your outlook on life in general. Implementing the ideas and methodology will transform you in unimaginable ways; enjoy the ride!

Step 1
Get in the Proper Mindset

First off, let's begin with the right mindset, meaning that you need to be at your most creative and able to think outside the box from the start. That will make it the easiest to start breaking down barriers to achieve your goals most effectively.

1. Sit back and relax.
2. Take a deep breath and hold it for 10 seconds.
3. Very slowly exhale.
4. Repeat numbers 1 through 3 three times.
5. Just let go of all preconceived ideas that you have on goal management.

It's always best to start any new endeavor from a place of calm and peace. Getting started on the right foot is one of the most critical steps to take.

Getting into the proper mindset will allow you to fully develop your TERM Analysis.

To fully develop your TERM Analysis, the proper mindset will allow you to think, feel, and act with deep personal freedom. To act from a place of purpose and value in your life.

- You will prioritize your activities better later.
- You will better identify where you are wasting money on your goals.
- When you spend your efforts and energy properly, you avoid burnout.
- Everything is interrelated; one always affects another. Remember this throughout the book.
- You will realize that you have more partners and resources than you thought possible

Step 2
Set Your Goal

This is going to be the focal point of your entire TERM analysis. As you will see, everything interrelates and spirals towards one thing, achieving your goal.

1. Always begin with the end in mind.
2. Make sure that you are clear on your goal.
3. Do not mix goals. For example, do not state that your goal is to lose 20 pounds and eat better. Focus, your goal is to lose 20 pounds, and eating better is an activity that will support this goal.

Tips to set help your goal

Your goal is the entire focal point of this analysis and is placed in the center. The tried and true SMART mnemonic to setting your goal is used to make it crystal clear.

- Specific - The clearer and more defined your goal is the better.
- Measurable - Put a number to it so that success and failure can be easily measured in the end.
- Action-Oriented - Be able to make movements immediately towards your goal, don't wait, don't hesitate.
- Rewarding - The goal should be rewarding to you in some way; personally, professionally, business-wise, or spiritually. This will keep you on track when bumps in the road occur.
- Time-bound - Put an end date on your goal, plain and simple, exactly when (day-date and time) will your goal be accomplished.

Having clearly set your goal upfront you have your target to focus on. You have your singularity that will drive the entire TERM analysis.

Step 3
The Time Quadrant

The first item to focus on is time. The how much, the when, the sequences throughout a typical day. Start thinking about time, not necessarily to manage it because time management does not work. Think of your target goal, and make sure that it is clear in your mind. Take a step back and look at your entire life and everything that you have going on.

1. How much time are you willing to dedicate towards achieving this goal every single day?
2. How much time every week?
3. …every month?
4. …every quarter? (if applicable)
5. …every year? (if applicable)
6. What time during the day are you most creative? Most productive?
7. When during each day/week/month, will you work on this goal completely focused and undeterred?

More About Working Your Time Quadrant.

The first item that throws you off track in your productivity journey is underestimating the amount of time that achieving your goal will take.

- Recognize that there is an end date by which your project or goal will be considered complete.
- It always takes longer to do something than anticipated, recognize this upfront, prepare for it mentally, and schedule it.
- Recognize as quickly as possible when you are falling behind in order to make proper adjustments.
- You must be able to come up with your top 3 priorities each day towards completing your goal.

Step 4
The Energy Quadrant

Your energy is like the gasoline in the tank of a car, the faster you hit the pedal, the quicker the gas will run out. Recognizing and being aware of how much energy you have and when your energy is flowing properly will help you recognize when you are best fit to work on your goal.

Ask yourself these questions to determine your energy Quadrant:

1. How much of my energy am I willing to put towards this goal?
2. When is my energy at its highest?
3. When is my energy low?
4. How long can I sustain my energy towards achieving this goal every day?

More About Your energy

Anything worthwhile in life is going to take a good amount of energy to accomplish. To avoid burnout, it is important to recognize your energy as a resource to be managed properly.

- Burnout must be avoided at all costs; it is the enemy of achieving your goal.
- Daily energy management is critical to your success.

A few tips to help manage your energy so that you can be at your very best when attacking your goal.

- Proper rest and sleep are critical.
- What you eat (fuel) is as important as how you eat and when you eat.
- How and when you practice proper breathing techniques matter.
- Exercise and exercise some more!
- The outlook is important.

Step 5
Resources Quadrant

You have more resources than you realize and there are more resources out there than you can imagine. Expand your mindset, be creative, and look around. Resources are anything and anyone that will help you achieve your stated goal. Some questions to ask about resources are:

1. Who will support me in this endeavor?
2. What information can I find to help me achieve this goal?
3. Where can I find industry knowledge to make learning faster?
4. Where can I find support for free?
5. Where can I find the support that will cost money?

More About Your Available Resources

People are one of the most valuable resources out there. Like a hammer, they can either build or destroy. Therefore, recognizing and finding the right people to support your goal is a top priority.

- Find an accountable person who will always support you, at any cost.
- Find a partner to help work towards the stated goal. A partner is someone that you can work with and might benefit from the goal's achievement.
- The authors of productivity books can make great partners and accountability coaches.

Another resource is the quality of the information that you receive to achieve your goal. There is information about everything out there, but the quality of that information might be outdated, to say the least. Double-check the source and date to decide the level of its quality in support of your goal.

- Search "how to...[topic]" and "[topic]...tutorial" on popular video sites for step by step instructions.
- Libraries, while dated at times, are still the go-to location for a place to study and think as well as finding support material.

Step 6
Money Quadrant

It takes money to make money, as the saying goes, and to a certain degree that is true. However, it shouldn't take a dollar to make 50 cents. This is what often happens when your goals and beliefs are not congruent with each other. Some things to consider when checking into your money quadrant:

1. How much money does your goal need to be achieved? (Not how much money do I need to achieve this as there is a huge difference that will be explored more later as the process interrelates.)
2. When does the first penny need to be placed towards your goal?
3. How often does money need to be injected into the process to achieve success?
4. Why does this cost so much?

More About Money

Unless you are the Central Bank, money is not infinite so it must be respected and allocated properly and in a timely manner.

- Make an initial budget towards achieving your stated goal from Step 2.
- Now add 50% to your original budget and that will most likely be the reality.
- Remember that unexpected costs always come up, be prepared for them.
- Create three to seven milestones where success can be measured, and payments made.
- Evaluate the status of the budget as frequently as possible daily and weekly are best.

Reminder, you can do more with less almost always. Lookout and protect your budget at any cost.

Step 7
Time Energy Relations

This is where it is going to get interesting and interlocked. There is only a certain amount of time and energy that can go towards your goal daily, so this must be accounted for.

1. How does your time and energy throughout the day flow?
2. When will you be most productive towards this one specific goal set in Step 2?
3. If a task takes more time than initially allocated, how will this affect energy the rest of your day?
4. If your goal tasks are finished earlier so there is extra time and good energy for the day, what next?

More About Time Energy Relations

An earlier end date was established for the stated goal and time allocated each day/week/month etc. towards achieving your goal. It is important to recognize now that maximum effort must be given during this time allocation towards achieving your goal.

- Make sure that you are at maximum effort and energy during the time you are working on your goal.
- Giving less effort now will result in more time lost later.
- The time of the day you are at peak productivity will help accelerate this process.

Time and energy are interconnected at their core and feed off one another constantly throughout life so it is better to recognize the health of this relationship upfront and manage it wisely to help goal achievement and productivity because you do not want this working against you.

Step 8
Energy Resources

Improper resources or the mismanagement of resources are some of the fastest ways to drain energy. Earlier you looked at energy and how important it is to be aware of when you are working at peak productivity.

1. Are the people resources you've identified taking energy away from you and your goal?
2. Does your support network energize you and make you feel better about your progress? It should. Always.
3. Does the place that you are working on your goals make you feel great about your progress?
4. Do the books, seminars, courses, videos, etc. add to your excitement about achieving your goal? Did they aid in the actual progress?

More About Energy and Resources

In the quest for hyper-productivity, resources should always be adding to your energy. Managing resources with the purpose of energy enhancement should be a top priority.

- If your accountability partner is draining your energy or you do not look forward to their help, cut them immediately, and find another one.
- Avoid the resource rabbit hole at all costs, if your attention starts to waver and you are not completely dialed into your goal, step away, and take a breath.

If you are feeling down or sluggish, look at how you have managed (or mismanaged) your resources the past few days, there will be your answer.

Step 9
Time Energy Resources

Everything is starting to come together. This is a process, working and reworking as you build everything up.

1.   Given the resources identified earlier, will they add or subtract energy from your quest, and how will this affect the time you have allocated?
2.   Is the time you have allocated towards your goal enough to keep your energy positive towards achieving this, and will your resources help you?

More About Time Energy Resources

Money and budget are purposely ignored at this point since the outcome is to focus on congruency of time, energy, and resources.

- Look at how your time is affected by the energy and resources put towards your goal.
- Think about what gives you energy towards your goals and how that helps you better allocate your time and what resources support you.
- Double-check that your resources support your energy and improve your time.

Money and budget will come back as a constraint, but first, you need congruency on the scope of what it will take to reach your goal.

Step 11
Resources & Money

Resources should not cost very much money, in fact, this part is to get you thinking about how little money you should invest in resources to start. This is to make sure that you are investing your budget towards your desired goal properly.

1. Does this resource cost additional money to support my goal?
2. Why is it necessary to NOT invest money into this resource?
3. If you must invest money into this resource, why is it necessary?
4. What higher-level function does this resource support?

The main reason for trying to NOT invest money is to stretch your thinking and look for support in places that are not obvious. You want to stretch yourself beyond what you think is possible and easy.

More About Resources & Money

Looking at all potentially available resources, and taking the time to think through the ones you do not have to invest extra money into, will help stretch your problem-solving skills towards the single focus of achieving your goals.

- Everything needed to achieve your goals is already there, sometimes hidden; open your mind to find it.
- You set a desired goal at the beginning that is important. This will help give you the will to achieve it.
- Expanding your level of thinking will make it easier to manage bumps in the road that will eventually come.

It is always best to be fruitful with the resources you have available. There are many support systems in place that are not readily seen, but once they are, they cannot be unseen.

Step 12
TERM

Your TERM quadrant is complete and now is the time to sit back and look at the entire picture. Until now you have focused on building the bits and pieces and how some of the parts interrelate and work together.

1. How does a change in time affect energy, resources, and money?
2. How does a change in energy affect time, resources, and money?
3. How will a change in resources affect time, energy, and money?
4. How will a change in money affect time, energy, and resources?

These questions are an interactive process and important to go through many times.

More About Your TERM

Your time, energy, resources, and money are the main quadrant spaces to achieve your goals. Most people do not properly prepare or set themselves up to make sure that their lives are congruent with their goals.

- Work on your TERM every single day
- Practice makes permanent, so make sure that the good is what is permanent.
- Have faith, you can do this.
- It is about taking action and making small consistent steps every day towards your goal.

Step 13
Bumps in the Road

The toughest part about any journey is the unexpected bumps in the road. These bumps will test you, set you back, and put you behind. They will make you doubt yourself.

Looking back at your Desired Goal and TERM Analysis ask yourself the following:

1. What bumps in the road can I expect?
2. What bumps in the road should I expect?
3. How will I overcome them?
4. How will a bump in time affect everything else?
5. How will a bump in energy affect everything else?
6. How will a bump in resources affect everything else?
7. How will a bump in money affect everything else?

More About Bumps in the Road

Have you ever been on a road trip somewhere
and not hit a pothole or speedbump?
You have done an excellent job stating your
desired goal and setting about all the time,
energy, resources, and money you will need to
achieve this goal. Now, just expect to hit bumps
in the road and prepare to overcome them as they
arise.

- You cannot plan for every possible
  situation so do not try.
- Prepare yourself emotionally that bumps
  occur, this analysis will help you adjust.
- Bumps can be the best learning
  experience that you haven't recognized
  yet.

Bumps will always be there, most often hidden,
but you can be mentally prepared to pivot and
swivel as needed to achieve your goals. Never let
them stop you. Bumps are there to help you grow.

Step 14
Focus

This entire TERM Analysis is designed to help you focus on the task at hand and what is truly important to attain your stated goal. This is why your goal is at the center of the analysis and why every part focuses back on this central issue, your goal. Always focus on it and do not let distraction get in your way.

1. What is taking your focus off your stated goal?
2. Who is taking your focus off your stated goal?
3. How can you quickly readjust to get yourself back on track?

More About Focus

A lack of focus in society today has hindered more personal growth and destroyed more dreams than any media source. Let that sink in, social media is only a distraction if you allow it to be one. Remember to look at your stated goal every day with the following in mind:

- Focus on your time.
- Be cognizant of the energy you are using.
- Recognize the resources available to you in all forms that are part of your support system.
- A lack of money will stretch your thinking to the possibilities.

Remember that everything interrelates with each other and that a slight imbalance in one area will have cascading effects on all other areas. Staying focused, steadfast, and strong in yourself and your commitment to your goals and ultimately your success will make you happier and stronger than you ever thought possible.

Step 15
Putting it all together

Your TERM Analysis, like everything in life, is fully and completely interconnected. The main reason that people do not reach their goals and are not more productive in life is that they are not fully committed and congruent towards achieving their goals.

1. Do you see how everything is interconnected here?
2. Is it easier to see how one quadrant will affect the other (positively or negatively)?
3. Can you see how adding or subtracting from one space throws off the balance of the others?
4. Can you see that there is a need for constant adjustments? And that's okay.

More About Putting it all Together

Your time, energy, resources, and money are the main quadrant spaces that have to be set up in order to achieve anything in life that you want. Anything from writing a book, to flying an airplane and everything you can imagine will require some amount of the four quadrants discussed in this book.

- You have the basis to achieve anything you desire.
- Addition in one quadrant can lead to subtraction in another.
- Subtraction in one quadrant can lead to an addition in another.
- Hyper-focus everything you have on your goal, you will achieve it.

Everything in life has a TERM, what's yours?

You've finished. Before you go...

Tweet/share that you finished this book.

Please star rate this book.

Reviews are solid gold to writers. Please take a few minutes to give us some itty bitty feedback.

ABOUT THE AUTHOR

Matt Malouf is a part-time investor and author with a professional degree in engineering.

Matt specializes in Traffic Management, Real Estate Investing in Latin America, and Productivity Projects. He is a spirited, outgoing, and fun-loving person who enjoys eating, traveling, gardening, and looking at real estate with his loving and supportive spouse and 5 children. He has been able to combine all these passions into a fun and lucrative side hustle to plan and prepare for a prosperous retirement.

Matt loves helping business owners and solo entrepreneurs better their lives through his patented TERM Methodology teachings and consulting. "Resilient and happy small business owners make for a better world. Not only today, but tomorrow as well, live long, prosper and be productive damnit!"

Other books by Matt Malouf:

22 Secrets to Success and Wealth Creation

Matt's Selling Your Home Resource Guide

Matt's Foreclosure Home Buying Secrets

Short Term Rental Success Stories from the Edge, Series

If you enjoyed this Itty Bitty® book
you might also like…

- **Your Amazing Itty Bitty® Fear Busting Book** – Lucetta Zaytoun

- **Your Amazing Itty Bitty® Achieving Your Potential** – Rena´ Koesler

- **Your Amazing Itty Bitty® Stress Reduction Book** – Denise Thomson, CHC

Or any of the many Amazing Itty Bitty® books available on line at www.ittybittypublishing.com

9 781950 326754